AVOIDING ORGANIZATIONAL CRIME METHODS

JOH LOK

Copyright

Contents

Preface

Introduction

Human had entered the 21 St century. It means that human will face challenges and we need to solve, if we hope our any dreams or goals can succeed. However, I believe that learning social knowledge , psychological knowledge can help us to achieve any short term goals or long term goals more easily. Because human existence needs to learn any kinds of new knowledge to help us to solve any challenges more easily. It explains that why we need to know psychological science. Although, any science is important to help our social development, e.g. space science, math, engineering, earth science, biology, medical science different subjects etc., but mathematicians will make judgement in error in possible. If math is only learning calculating knowledge, but it does not need and without human's creative and logic mind activities in our learning process. We can not cause including math knowledge system. So, social psychological science can assist any subjects to help human to create any new kinds of knowledge to solve any challenges to achieve any new directions for our social any benefits more easily.

Nowadays, technological development causes there are many businessmen who need to use internet to co-operate their businesses from internet transaction. It will cause employees have chance to use technological methods to steal employers whose cash from whose companies' computer system. So, if whose employers neglect to concern whose employees' behavior. It will have company's loss threats from whose employees' crime behavior in possible.

Thus, if employers can permit when those employees' stealing crime behavior will occur or who will be the first one or next one business crime behavior staff or where the business crime place in whose office or store or shop or warehouse anywhere places or locations are. Then, I believe that the businessmen whose loss threats will be reduced from staffs' stealing ensure.

This book aims to be given my opinions to let businessmen can apply psychology methods or minds or technological methods to predict staff when whose will act business crime psychology behavior when and where will occur in any situations more easily. Because if any one businessman who has good business analysis and logic mind. Then, whose business loss will possible reduce to the minimum level. So, this book is suitable to any businessmen to learn how to predict when and where and who will do insider's theft behavior. Also, crime psychology students can learn new crime concepts to raise crime psychology knowledge.In my this book, I shall explain what psychological functions can help our society to raise more benefits in possible and my readers can begin to know why we need have psychological knowledge to learn.

I write this topic aims to explain where working environment may cause employees attempt to steal any office things or warehouse products or any working places things more easily, what factors encourage employees do stealing crime behaviors , why employees themselves have stealing crime psychological behaviors, as well as I shall gives suggestion whether employers ought how to do in order to encourage their employees do stealing crime behaviors in any working places more easily as well as I shall explain what methods may help employers may know or judge whom employees are planning to do stealing crime behaviors more accurately. This book is suitable to crime psychology readers to research this office stealing issue.

Prologue

Table of content

Criminal behavioral psychological casing factors

Reference

ONE

WHAT IS PSYCHOLOGICAL FUNCTION

In general, psychology science is often mislead to explain what its functions wrongly by our society. Psychology English is come from " psyche" and " logos" two words consist. The prior word means " soul" and the later word means " theory" . So, psychological science is explanation of mind science. It is one kind of research human mind activities science or it is one kind of research human's behavioral science. Any kinds of human's Behaviors mean observation from environment influences. But, nowadays, psychological science of new explanation means human's mind and behavior observation both aspects research.

So, what does psychological science mean? In fact, anyone can be one part time (folk psychologist) . For example, any one child can own ability or knows how to predict any one's psychology or mind successfully, e.g. he knows how to keep his toy in not easy discovered or secret location in his house or school or any places, and he aims to make wrong direction to mislead his friends need to spend much time to find his toy. He aims to achieve none any his friends or patents can find or discover this toy easily consequently. It explains that any one adult , even child, he does not need to be taught, but he can have himself mind or ability to feel whether he ought need to how to do himself behavior to achieve his aim immediately. This kind of personal creative or own protective behavior or mind research that is psychologists want to find any answers to support and to explain why and how child can own this kind of psychological mind. It is one part of psychological research aim.

Why does psychologists know what you want easily or they can make more accurate judgement? In general, psychologists feel need to do any psychological science research aims, because they want to discover or find what are the thinking or mind about any one in order to make the absolute accurate judgement. Psychologists' duties need to research any one's psychological activities, why he/she feel happy or sad or satisfactory or any emotion, which factors influence he/she Has this kind of emotion and what the relationship is between of them. For example, the person assumes that he often feels difficult to sleep, he will attempt to buy any useful drugs or medicines to eat to help him to sleep easily. But, if he can not still feel that any kinds of drug can help him to feel enough sleeping after he eats it easily. Then, he has possible to find one psychologist to help him to find what factors cause him to feel difficult to sleep. SO, finding any factors to cause any one feels disappoint or failure or fear or difficult to do any thing etc. different negative emotion challenges, it may be any psychologist's duty to know how to find the main factor(s) to help to serve his patients satisfactorily.

Some people feel psychologists' duties are easy. It is wrong view point. In fact, they need spend long time to research any psychological topics and they are very difficult to research in order to conclude any results or answers.

I shall indicate both interesting cases , they concern how psychologists can help their patients successfully as below:

For bind people example, some bind or without enough eye sight seeing any thing people who can not see any thing long time, some psychologists can help them to see any things clearly when they are old age successfully in possible.

For another horse lotto win money participates case, there is one group people decides to invest money to participate this time horse lotto winning money competition. Before, every time horse competition, they share their opinions to concern every time horse lotto competition. And then, they will concentrate nervous to discuss and make group participation final decision to choose which numbers of horses, they decide to buy together. For every horse lotto competition, it has these three kinds of different level of decisions. The first kind is the least risk and prudential decision, it is without any investment money is needed to buy any hour number in the horse lotto competition. The another more risk decision is invested less money to some horses , they feel that they have possible to race in win and the final is the most risk decision is that to invest less money to some horses only, but they do not know that they have no possible to win money in the time horse lotto race competition with every participant personal average opinion comparison.

So, the participant's overall final decision may include three results: (1) more prudential decision result, (2) more risk decision result (3) without more prudential and more risk decision result.

So, psychologists can attempt to help them to apply psychological concept and theory to give recommendation how to raise chance to win this horse race lotto competition before he had gathered any horse past race experience and winning or lose times information to analyze every horse's winning chance rate. However, the psychologist must not guarantee they can win any horse race lotto in this competition. He can only give suggestion to help them to make more accurate judgement whether they ought choose which number of horse to buy.

What investigation methods as used by psychological science? For example, researching about how much violence level to the movie, you need to do surveys to enquire any participants whose feeling to this violence movie. Your investigating method is survey method. For another example, your participation to research the patients eat the drug how to influence their feeling or emotion, it is drug laboratory experiment method. For final example, you participate the activity and the psychologists use video camera to record your behavior, it is one observation method.

Some psychologists apply experiment psychological method to find what the main factors influence the student feels bore or difficult to learn anything. Some psychologists apply physical psychological method to find what factors cause close relationship between building biology process (stage) and human behaviors, e.g. How do our brains carry on analyzing our daily activities? Where are our brain part locations for our emotion, activity and mind leading functions? Has it same brain activity to learn between reading English and reading Chinese language? Some psychologists apply development psychological method to research how and why human's character causes and personal psychological mind development process, social behavioral development. Hence, psychological science research may be our whole person life development process research. From student stage, we have chance to encounter learning difficulties, when working age stage, we may encounter challenge how to cooperate to work with team members efficiently in any organizations, till to our old age stage, we may encounter our psychological and mental and physical health challenge. Hence, psychologists need to apply their professional psychological knowledge to help us to solve our any personal challenges , when we have chance to encounter in our different life stages

- What is psychological mind analysis function

Do you feel that your behaviors will be influenced by non-control or unknown factors influence? Do you ensure that your behaviors are careless causes? Psychological analysis function can be applied to these aspect: It can help us to know what myself actual ability owning to do any matters. For example, because we feel happy, so we will feel that we have this kind of ability to do this matter, even it is difficult to let us to feel to finish. Because happy feeling motivate us to attempt to do this matter, but it does not represent that we must own this kind of effort to succeed to finish this matter. It is only ourselves personal ability feeling or we have no own this kind of ability in fact. Otherwise, actual myself ability is between myself ability and exceeding myself super ability; actual myself ability represents logic and clever or talent that you own, they you're your protective ability. We can follow actual principles to choose to attempt to do any matters in order to achieve satisfactory feeling.

So, when we know what is actual ourselves abilities own, we will have more chance to finish the matter successfully. Because we have known whether what our actual abilities own to do the matter to achieve more successful chance. The final psychological mind analysis is that when we know what our social principle is and our life aim or goal or intention is, then we won't limit out actual owning abilities to attempt to achieve our any life aims or goals successfully in the end our life.

For example, some talent scientists, talent musicians, talent actors. They had known what their actual abilities in their life own. SO, they can have more confidence to attempt to do " exceeding themselves abilities behaviors" to achieve their life goals successfully. They have these personal characteristics: They had correct or right psychological mind analysis to know whether what they real need or hope to achieve as well as what their actual themselves " super owning abilities" that they ensure to own in order to accept to spend long time to learn how to raise their unique skills or techniques as well as doing owning super ability behaviors to achieve their life dreams. For some space scientists, actors, super sport people their abilities are seemed to own god helping, their super abilities are due to they had known whether what their unique owning abilities are different to general humans. So, psychological mind analysis function aims to let any people attempt to find or discover whether they have any unique abilities , they are unknown and psychologists need to help them to attempt to find any unique abilities in order to create their talent skills or techniques in possible.

What is behavioral mind?
In general, in our living environment, we attempt to apply basic learning principle to change our behaviors. It is very common situation. We can observe someone's behaviors in order to learn their skills. For learning basket ball , football playing sport skills example, the basket ball , football players must not need the basket ball, football coach leaders to teach them how to play. They can observe any one football or basket ball team players to learn how their skills to play in proficient very easily. They only need to spend long time to observe their skills in order to learn their skills in success. It is observation learning method, though these observations in order to learning their abilities in success. It is one interesting topic to psychologists' research concerns whether we can observe any person's skills or techniques in order to learn their same level skills or techniques in success.

The question is that whether observation is right or wrong learning behavior or method to any leaners. It is general psychologists have interest to research topic. In general, they believe that our behaviors can be caused by external and internal both factors. The potential environment seems to everyone to be same, but actual environment is ourselves behaviors how are created. For example, one meeting environment people treat themselves attitudes are the same, but one person behaves more rude and not polite and causes noise feeling in whole meeting environment, so his not polite behavior influences the meeting environment people treat him more punishment, but less appreciation. Otherwise, any other people perform their

same behaviors , such as polite and quite personal attitude in the meeting environment. So , many people can create more appreciation, but less punishment behaviors between them in whole meeting environment. It means that we can create chance to ourselves in different environment. It depends on whether how we perform our behavior and feeling to adapt the different environment needs. Such as this meeting environment, when many people perform their behaviors to like to listen other people what they are speaking in quiet personal attitude and they are polite to let any one speak to express his/her opinion in prior in the whole meeting environment. So, these kind of personal behavioral performance attitude is accpeted to whole members. Otherwise, the only one member, he often performs himself behaviors to argue and rude attitude and he also performs not like to listen any one personal opinion, he only

believe his opinion must be the best among all of these members in whole meeting. So, he won't be appreciated his opinion performance and he will have punishment feeling from other members as well as he often feels arguement and he needs to spend much time to argue and support his opinions to other members' opposite opinions

in whole meeting process. Hence, in general any environment, we will be influenced to decide whether we ought choose to do ourselves behaviors in order to satisfy others people's acceptance more easily. Such as this meeting environment example, when some members feel their behaviors are appreciated or accepted , due to their performance and attitude are polite , liking acceptance to listen other opinions, without causing noise and argument, without performing perosnal attitude to let other feel himself/herself opinion must the best among all memebers. In this meeting members' discussion time, this kind of polite and liking listening, liking acceptance other opinions

personal attitude behavior will be appreciated. So, many memebers will feel to be appreciated among of them. Otherwise, the one member often perform rude and not polite personal attitude, and he only
likes others listen his opinion before anyone. He only feel that his opinion must be the best among of all members. However, he does not like to change his attitude to accept to listen other opinions before, he likes to cause arguement to discuss their opinions among of them and his behavior will let many members to feel rude. Due to he does not like accept to change his behavior in whole meeting environment. SO, he must feeling to be punished and without any appreciation in whole meeting
environment.

Hence, our behaviors ought be controlled or dominated by extrenal environment more than ourselves mind control if we hope our behaviors are accepted by many people in society in general. For example, if many the school class students hope to exam to pass this time examination more easily. Their mind will tell them that they will fail the time examination more easily, if they can not spend much time, e.g. one day spends at least 5 to 10 hours maximum per day and three months at least studying period to study hardly at home or school library. Then this class may have more than 50 percent students number will like to attempt to spend at least 5 hours hard to spend study in this three months studying period before this examination in order to achieve passing this examination successful aim or goal or intention.

So, this class student themselves mind is dominated by this classroom learning environment factor influence to persuade their hard studying learning
behavior. However, some lazy students will choose their

mind more than learning environment acceptance, so they will still choose to spend less than 5 hours per day and it is only one month or two month studying period to carry on studying to follow their learning time table daily. Because they
do not feel that they will have high chance to pass this examination if they can spend longer time and longer learning period to gather any
information or teaching material from their school library as well as reducing leisure time and increasing studying time at home before this examination.
So, it explains that somethimes we need to choose to accept to follow to do any decision from either ourselves mind or our external environment as well as we also need to make judgement whether what factor will bring more benefit to us after we choose to do our final decision from either ourselves mind or our external environment factor influence. Because we do not know that whether ourselves mind or acceptance general external environment public mind which can help us to achieve our any goals more easily. So, it explains that why sometimes we needs to do psychological mind analysis between acceptance to ourselves mind more or acceptance to general public mind more in order to implement or
achieve some decisions more success consequently.

IN conclusion, on psychologists psychological mind analysis view points, they need to help patients to know how and why whether they ought follow external environment public mind more
or themsleves mind more in order to judge whether their patients' choice to be decided to do same matters whether it is right or wrong judgement, when their patients feel difficult

to do some decisions and they need their recommendation to indicate their psychological mind anlaysis assistance need in order to achieve their any decisions more success.So, psychological mind analysis function aims to help patients to know or find reasons tro explain that why they ought choose to do the kind of behaviors and help them to judge whether their behaviors choice or decision is right or wrong to be accepted to general society, even themselves.

TWO

PSYCHOLOGIST SOCIAL SERVICE KINDS OF ASSISTANCE

In our society, we have many different kinds of psychologists, e.g. criminal psychology, child , young, old age psychology, education psychology,

adult psychology, patient psychology, mental psychology, adult psychology, mental psychology, employee organizational psychology etc. However,

different psychologists will have themselves different psychological service to satisfy their patient mental health needs. In this chapter, I shall

introduce these different kinds of psychologists' tasks how to satisfy their patients' mental health needs. I shall indicate these different kinds

of psychologists' tasks how to satisfy their patients' mental health psychological needs. I also indicate some cases to explain what their tasks differences are.

Firstly, in psychology at work or organizational behavior or employee employee psychological research aspect, it concerns a large part of how people define who they are is by what they do. Work can be a key part of our social identity to build employees sense of themselves. IN special, employees organizational psychology
helpe organizations to solve employees mental health and how to bring a good job satisfactory feeling and it can promote psychological wellbeing when people are employed have lower rates of psychological health problems group target.

In psychology at work research aspect, it includes these organizational psychological assistance aspect: How to create a psychological healthy workplace to a meaningful work and what can keep people fulfilled and productive in their jobs ? It considers how to let employees to feel how to do work more attrative, rather than how to
make unemployment less attractive. As well as how improving on physical health and sickness absence to some lazy employees' negative mind psychological influence, how the organizational
psychological health of the workforce impacts on organizational health of the organizational performance, how to help organizations measure optimal levels of engagement at work
have significant benefits for the employee. Such higher levels of engagement are characterised by increased levels of angry, dedication, being strongly involved in one's work, experienccing a sense of significance, and being absorbed in one's work so time passes quickly.

So, how to designing work to encourage engagement is also needed to bring beneficial to the employers, helping organizations to attempt to find whether what of a number of key factors influence employees' psychological health and wellbeing in the workplace as well as seeking why and how some individual factors are other are linked to the work environment, e.g. finding what the main reason(s) whether it is/ they are the job insecurity or dissatisfaction or increased risk of low engagement or poor rewarded or long working hours time or feeling boreing etc. different factors influence a decreased productivity to bring a negative impact on the organization's employees.

Hence, employee organizational psychologists need to give their professional opinions to serve any organzations to help them to find what the main factor(s) influence(s) some or all employees' productive performance is(are) caused poor suddenly as well as finding the effective solutions or methods to attempt to help the organizations to recover or improve or raise their employees' productive performance effectively and efficiently in order to achieve the consequence to let all employees will feel happy or feel satisfactory to work in the organizations to avoid employees leaving turnover number increasing occurrence in possible.

Secondly, in concerning mental health and distress preventive psychology aspect, mental health psychologists need to let feeling mental distress hospital patients feel their mental disease or mental pressure can be changed to be health in possible. They need to help any mental patients to find what factors cause their mental sickness (illness), e.g. their mental sicknesses are caused from job stress or personal negative emotion, focus on distress or prior personal sad or unhappy past life experience. THeir mental health service aims to help their mental patients to solve any mental health problems are either illnesses or diseases.

All these mental illnesses are assumed by a focus on distress as something
that is perhaps " in the mind". So, all mental illness patients , their mental illnesses are assumes to have cause and effect relationship to their " poor mind" illnesses.

SO, mental health psychologists will focus on their mind research to find why and how they have any mental illnesses suddenly. The term mental illness, for example, any mental
health psychologists will suggest that their walk will be illness, and it has a medical character, but that ill will also take a mentalistic or psychological focus. It is the different between a mental health psychologist and a nervous illness doctor how they view their mental illness patients, e.g. a nervous illness doctor will suggest the right
medicine (drug) to attempt to help the mental illness patient, but a mental health psychologist will apply psychological knowledge to attempt to help the mental illness patient to solve his mental problems. So, the mental health psychologist will feel psychological health treatment is more useful to compare medicine oe drug eating treamtment, and they will assume that the mental patient's problems is caused due to his psychological emotion factor more than his physical illness factor. For example, one person feels distress or mental pressure, mental health psychologist will feel his distress may be caused from overload job pressure, but a vervous illness doctor will feel his pressure is caused
by body physical illness factor more than poor or negative emotion influencing factor. So, one mental health psychologist is one mental health psychologist doctor to find whether what external environment or his/her personal psychological emotion is his main factor to cause

his patient feels unpleasant or emotion pressure feeling suddenly in
order to solve his psychological illness problem successfully.

Hence, medical psychologists are well aware of the close link between physical disease and mental health. Frequently, psychologists are asked to see a patient who has been admitted to a general medical facility , due to a medical illness or disease that may have a psychological overlay. When providing clinical services to a medical patient in a general hospital, psychologists are finding that they are part of an interdisciplinary team. IN conclusion, any hospitals or clinics must nee medical
psychologists give medical psychological methods to solve patients‘ psychological challenges when he/she feels disappointed or fear himself or herself will die in possible in order to avoid he/she commits suicide easily. Hence, medical psychologist needs to help any patients to build positive emotion continue alive independence. Their role needs to assist
doctors to solve their patients' psychological health needs when they are living in hospitals, even they leave their hospitals in future one day.

Thirdly, for crininal psychology social function aspect, why does our society need criminal psychologists? IN our legal system of our society , it is a reflection of what is considered tolerable and intolerable behavior within that particular society, i.e. intolerable behavior is disapproved of by the majority. However, we must have people to
anti-social behavior to let our sosciety to know their dissatisfaction, it is their criminal intent major factor. IN fact, any legally wrong or immoral behavior , e.g.

burglary, fraud , killing theft, trespass, fighting are caused by the criminal people's negative psychological factor. In general, although many of them had known that they will be punished if they still do criminal behaviors in our society. But, they can not dominate or control themselves to do any criminal behaviors. So, it explains why that we still need criminal psychologists to help them to find why they do criminal behavioral reasons after they had done criminal behaviors as well as
they are punished to go to court to be judged consequently.

Criminal psychologists aim to let their criminal patients to know their errors and use professional acriminal psychological methods to help them to learn how to avoid to do any criminal behaviors again after they are free to go to society to prepare to find new jobs to do or beginning re-new life again. The criminal psychologists will make
a number of assumptions that any criminal people who have these similar characteristics. They may include as below:

The first assumption is that every individual's behaviors is due to their own interpretation of reality and real environment can influence how any why the person does criminal behavior in society.
The second assuption is that people will learn meaning by observing how other people react in society , both positively and negatively. SO , if the person often contact his friends who often react
negative social behavior, they will influence or persuade him to trend to do any criminal behavior more easily in society. The third assumption is that we evaluate our own behaviors according
to the meanings, we have learned and that we have acquired from others. So, we will learn any one's behavior and we

will make evaluation whether we ought or ought not follow their behaviors
to do. For example, any one knows killing another person is a criminal act. However, in some suitations, for instance, when a peson kills in self-defence, when a legitimate killing because he needs to protect himself body to be attacked to cause hurt, even death as well as he feels that he has possible to be killed if he does not decide to kill the person in the environment immediately. So, criminal psychologists needs to help the killer to feel that he is not a actual killer in psychological view point, although he had killed the person in legal view point in orde to avoid that he commits suicide himself easily in any time.

Hence, any one criminal psychologist, he/she had learnt these criminal psychological knowledge to prepare how to help his / her owning criminal mind and doing criminal behavioral patients to solve negative psychological or negative emotion challenge after they had done criminal activites. Their criminal psychological knowledge
may include these several aspects: Knowledge of key concepts and psychological models of criminal behavior, capacity to identify the different perspective on human nature under the theoretical
development and research of any criminal behavioral causes, familiarity with research methodologies commonly employed in the field of criminal psychology, as well as a
capacity for analyzing their strengths and weaknesses , a biosocial fame of reference included, ability to examine critically specific offences and apply psychological models of
criminality to case studies, awareness of the different prevention, treatment strategies for working with offenders, a range of presentation skills. They need to do

face to face contact to
spend some time, e.g. one day one to two hours, five days within every week time to talk to the criminal person is prison in order to find whether whar his/her negative psychological or negative emotion factor(s) can cause or influence his/her decision to make any kinds of criminal activities consequently as well as finding the methods to let they feel positive emotion or positive psychological reflection to avoid to do any similar criminal activities again after he/she leave the prision in orde to protect our social safety, due to their criminal activities occurrence again and reducing criminal rate raising occurrence easily in our society .

Forthly, I will explain what the educaiton psychological function is. Education psychologists may give recommendation to teachers how to encourage their students to themselves learning interest to be raised by their teachers' teaching methods influence or themselves psychological learning method influence both as well as how to improve their school classrooms teaching -learning environment in order to influence their students feel happy to learn in their classrooms to achieve aim to help them to get high grade results consequently. It is helpful in instructional strategies and provides basis for the selection of appropriate methods, techniques, approaches , tools to satisfy
and fulfil the need of learners that results in better learning, with the help of educational psychological teacher is able to create positive learning environment in the clasrooms resulting in effective learning. So, the educational psychologist plays an important role in making learning easy, joyful and interesting process. Likewise also conflict classroom management strategies may be used in teaching,

learning leading towards better ways of delivering information to the learners in the classroom.

Finally, I shall explain what child psychology is? Every child stage development is important to influence his/her personal behavior when he/she grows up to be adult. So, child psychologists need to give opinions to their any ons child patient's partents and help their every child patient's patients to know why to teach their child/children in positive

teaching and learning way, when they are living at home daily. Because every child whose patients wll influence his/her behavior when he/she is adult and he /she needs to work in society.

For example, how to create or develop the child's unique skill or technique if the child is one one talent child to be needed to find whether he/she owns which kinds of skills , which

need their patients help him/her to discover. Then the child can concentrate on training to upgrade the kind of undiscovered skills to hel him/her to become one talent child as well as attributing his/her human intelligence to our society's benefit. For another example, the educational psychologist needs to give opinions to the child's parents to teach

them how to persuade the child to follow learning disciplines to raise learning ability when they contact at home, the child ought first to be presented with problems and methods and only later with disciplines.

In conclusion, all of above these different kinds of psychologists, they have different professional psychological knowledge and skill to help our

social different stakeholder patients to solve their mental problems and satisfy their mental health service nees in

order to let our society can
have many positive psychological mind people feel happy to live in our society.

THREE

DEFINITION OF CRIME BEHAVIOR

In psychology, there are three theories to explain crime behavior. First is the consensus view, which indicates the legal system of the society is a reflection of what is considered tolerable and intolerable behavior within particular society, i.e. intolerable behavior is disapproved of by the majority. Before a crime can be said to have occurred, it has to be committed. So, without an action, there can be no crime. The act must be legally forbidden. It is not enough to just be anti-social behavior, and the act must also have a criminal intent to commit to act. For example, if a banker helps the bank's client to invest to cause loss, carelessly, who has not proved to help whose client to invest to cause loss intentionally. Then, who has no criminal intent to commit the act. The staff's behavior must be legally wrong, may not be morally wrong only. For example, the bank teller is proved to steal whose bank employer's clients' saving account money for himself/herself to steal to use. This is legally wrong behavior. Otherwise, the bank teller neglect to help the bank clients to keep to save box carefully. Then, it is morally wrong behavior, because who has no intentional stealing behavior. Thus, business crime needs the person has crime behavior, not only moral in behavior only. Second is the conflict view, it is the direct opposite of the consensus view. In society, some group of people believe different groups of people, such as students, professionals, unions, businessmen etc. These groups are in conflict with each other in a range of ways, due to the inequality of the way that wealth is divided. There will be some poorer people, some wealthier people, some power, some with no power. Thus inequality leads to a society based on conflict, which is thought to then promote crime. For example, poorer people, e.g. no job people or unemployed people who will commit crimes, such as theft, burglary, murder, when middle class people may commit crimes, such as theft from employers when collar crime, fraud. The upper classes may commit crimes such as environmental pollution, and damage which may not be considered crime in same way as burglary, for example. Third is the interactionist view, it maintains that there is no moral right or wrong, rather changes in moral standards affect the legal standards. For example, killing another person is a criminal act. However, in some situations, for instance, when a person skills in self-defense, it is considered as legitimate killing.

What are social psychological crime reasons? Why does working environment influence staff individual crime decision? What do legal procedure strike staffs as fair? In criminal cases, psychological factors may influence decisions involving arrest, prosecution, bargaining etc. criminal behavior.

When making arguable social judgement, e.g. whether the staff have crime intent to do whose behavior, it means innocent behavior, e.g. stealing office cash or computer's behavior. Would this defendant commit such as offence or intentionally? Facts are not all that matter. In the types of staff's individual crime, in the status, age, sex and race of the defendant, it's hard to isolate the factors that influence the employer's judge. The fact includes physical attractiveness, for example, when employers asked individual staff to judge the guilt of baby -aced and mature-faced of the staff defendant. The Baby-faced adult (staff with large, round eyes and small chins) seemed most native and were found guilty more often of crimes of negligence and less often of intentional criminal acts in office. It convicted, unattractive staffs also strike people as more dangerous, especially if who are sexual offenders in working environments.

Any ethical concern is about scientific jury selection, experiments reveal that the staff individual attitudes and personal characteristics don't always predict how and when and why whose crime behavior caused. There are no magic questions to be asked, not even a guarantee that a particular survey will detect that a particular survey will detect useful to the criminal staff individual attitude-behavior and personality-behavior relationship for whose criminal intention.

Does the criminal staff who subject to the social influence to cause whose criminal behavior decision in office? e.g. stealing office cash or computer or any office properties . For example, a bank counter staff steals whose bank employer whose withdraw one client's saving account money to provide himself/herself to use or doing false office documents to earn personal bank loan borrowing benefits for whose one bank client to earn personal benefit illegal behavior.

To patterns of either minority influence, or even to majority group staffs think to do office criminal behavior. All in office environment, one individual staff who has criminal intention, usually who is usually by minority or majority group influence by whose colleagues. It is possible that who decide to plan to do office criminal stealing behavior together. So, when the staff steals the valuable thing in office, who will sell the valuable thing to exchange interest to share this illegal cash earns with whose colleagues to enjoy together. Thus, although it seems that this stealing behavior is belong to this staff one person to do, but the fact, it is possible the minority or majority group colleagues had planned to arrange when and how and where to encourage who have confidence to attempt to do this criminal behavior in the office first time. Because who feels whose employer won't know who will steal this office property and when this office property will be stolen and where any office property will be stolen. However, it is a hypothetical situation to let this office staff and whose other colleagues to feel whose employer doesn't know this stolen matter will happened. So, it causes who have more confidence to attempt to do this stealing criminal psychological behavior in office. Otherwise, if who feel whose employer will know this stealing matter will happen. It means that the employer will know who will steal his one kind of property and where this property is located and when this property will be stolen in office. Then, I believe who don't choose to attempt to plan to do this criminal stealing behavior in office.

Is the process to motivate the staff's criminal behavior by which certain minority or majority group of the staff individual colleagues and to guide or persuade him/her to encourage whom to attempt to whose stealing criminal behavior in office? One example of the power of the staff individual criminal behavior in office is leadership. The process by which is certained the individual staff is mobilized and is guided by whose minority or majority colleagues group in office. Some office leaders are formally appointed or elected by their minority or majority colleagues group in office; others emerge informally as the criminal group interacts in office. What makes for good office criminal group leadership often depends on the situation, the best colleague relationship person (staff) to lead the criminal colleagues team may not make the best criminal leader of the sales force, e.g. criminal stealing office property behavior. Some staffs excel or task leadership at criminal organizing work, setting criminal guide and focusing on criminal goal attainment in office. Others excel at social leadership, at building criminal teamwork, mediating solving conflicts and being supportive with colleagues (staffs) in office.

In office, social leaders (criminal behavior leaders) often have a democratic style, one that delegates authority and welcomes input from criminal staff team members in office. Many experiments reveal that such leadership is good for morale, e.g. office morale. To office, minority or majority colleagues group criminal behavioral members who usually feel more satisfied when who participate in making criminal behavioral decisions in office. If a office criminal behavioral leaders can control or plan or lead over whose criminal behavioral task or steps, the team of criminal colleagues also become more motivated to achieve stealing behavior more successful in office. So, the office criminal behavioral leaders who value good criminal behavioral team feeling and take pride in achievement therefore criminal behavior is encouraged to cause under democratic leadership. Any effective office criminal leadership styles, we now know, vary with the situations in office environments. So, the most effective office criminal supervisors in coal mines, banks and government organizations etc. environmental offices score high on tests of both criminal task and social relationship. They are actively concerned for how criminal work is progressing and sensitive to the criminal behavioral needs of their subordinates in office. Thus, it will encourage office criminal behavior causing more easily. Studies also reveal that many effective office criminal leaders of laboratory groups, work teams, and large corporations exhibit office criminal behaviors that promote or encourage minority or majority colleagues to influence criminal behaviors occur in office. Otherwise, sometimes, to be sure, office criminal teams also influence their criminal leaders. In trying to under staffs, employers wonder why who act and way to do criminal or immoral behavior in office. For example, if worker productivity declines, does the employer assume the workers are getting lazier? Or has their equipment become less efficient? When a salesperson says that outfit really looks nice on the client, does this reflect genuine feeling or telling immoral lie to give wrong message to persuade the client to feel this shirt is beautiful or comfortable when who wears it to choose to buy misleading.

It is attributing causality to the staff or the working situation. Employer endlessly analyze and discuss why office immoral, even criminal behaviors happen as who do, especially when something negative or unexpected occurs. Attribution theory analyzes how we explain people's behavior, such as how employers explain staffs' behavior. The variations of attribution theory share some common assumptions that we (employers) seek to make sense of our world (office environment), then we (employers) attribute people's (staff's) individual actions to internal or to external causes, and that we (employers) do so in fairly logical, consistent ways.

The theory of how people (staffs) explain others' (colleagues') behavior, for example, by attributing, it either to internal dispositions (enduring traits, motives and attributes) or to external situations in office. Such as, in office environment, these three factors, consistency, distinctiveness and consensus influence whether the staff (criminal behavior leader) attributes colleague's individual criminal behavior to internal or external causes in office. First, consistency factor indicates that: Does the staff usually behavior this criminal behavior (way) in this situation ? Second, distinctiveness factor indicates that: Does the staff behave differently in different situations in office environments? Third, consensus factor indicates that: Do other colleagues behave similarly in this situation in this office environment? Thus, it seems, office environment is one external factor to cause the staff's criminal behavior occurrence in office as well as the staff internal factor, e.g. feeling no people discover or know whose criminal behavior is carrying in office, so whose feeling can motivate who have confidence to attempt to do whose criminal or immoral behavior in office.

How can employers prevent crime and misconduct in whose business from staffs' immoral or criminal behavior in working environment? Nowadays, investing in crime and misconduct prevention tends to be more financially advantages rather than setting losses after staff's individual criminal behavior has occurred. So, corporate security protects the company's business activities, interest groups, data and property from human error, misconduct and criminal intent. To support their efforts, to establish a secure environment, companies need information about criminal practices and methods of safeguarding themselves. However, small and medium sized companies invest all too little in risk-reducing measures. The reasons for this can often be found in limited available resources and a lack of awareness about the types of crime and other threats who may be facing. Otherwise, the largest companies clearly invest the most in measures to reduce potential security risks. However, a notable higher number of crimes and acts of misconduct are directed at large companies.

In global , the majority of companies rely on technical security measures. However, companies should invest in security training in addition to technical solutions, because training in addition to technical solutions, because security fail as a result of intentional or deliberate actions made by personal. Information leaks can also be reduced through training. If the company has not provided any guidance in formation management, then the easiest way to gain access to confidential company information may simply be any contacting one of its employees.

In fact, by global statistic showed that half of the companies had not trained their personnel in how to handle confidential information. A though employee recruiting process, including background checks, assists in developing corporate security. These processes help the company to reduce the security risks related to its personnel and ensure that a staff is suitable for the task who is being hired to perform.

Nowadays, attempted crimes and acts of misconduct are often directed at company records and files. The most common breaches involved attempts at unauthorized entry into the company's data network. In large companies, the number of attempts at unauthorized entry has higher than the average. The risk/ threats related to data security include: attempts of unauthorized entry or hacking into the data network, copying information for one's own use prior to leaving the service of the company, unauthorized disclosing of critical corporate information to a third party, unauthorized snooping into corporate records or files (content), intentional destruction of files, unauthorized entry or hacking into the data network, unauthorized surrendering of confidential corporate documents to a third party and unauthorized altering/ false of corporate records of files (content) etc. stealing company's confidential data criminal behavior. Every company has information that needs to be protected. However, confidential information about a company can be leaked to an external party with deliberate intent. In every fifth company, an employee had copied internal company data prior to moving to another company within the same field of business. The chance of that confidential business information may be sent to competitors and may significantly harm a company's business activities from which staff's individual criminal behavior.

In order to define a crime as it relates to business secrets and to acquire the appropriate legal safeguards, the company must determine which information might be considered as secret, establish instructions for handling confidential. Besides, the risks/threats related to property may also include: theft of tools or equipment, forced entry into an office or production facility, vandalism of an office or production facility, significant loss. For example, many construction companies has experienced unauthorized entries into offices and production facilities. The greatest loss of material is experienced in construction and trade field. In order to reduce loss, companies can utilize a wide variety of technical security systems and security guard services in order to protect property. Moveable property is well marked and protected. Moreover, in order to reduce the risks, companies should need to invest in training and determining the human risk factors. For example, the use of a monitoring system requires that personnel acquaint themselves with the procedures required by the systems. Also, the threats of violence were clearly more common than actual acts of violence, since every third company states that their employees had experienced threats at work. Violent or threatening situations arose in connection with, among others, meetings with drunk or intoxicated customers or in different burglary, seizure or petty larceny situations. The risk of violence is increased when an employee works alone or late at night. To some extent, violence can be reduced through training and technical safety measures. Monitoring equipment also assists often security threats because of their company's activities or field of business. Among the large companies, every eighth stated that key personnel or their families had been threaten . The risks /threats related to personnel may include: an employee has been threaten at work; an employee has committed a crime/ acts of misconduct against your company; another type of work-related crime toward an employee has occurred; key personal or their families have received threats in relation to their work; an employee has been victim of violence at work; an employee has committed a crime/act of misconduct against your clients.

Thus, I recommend that management needs to show the direction. The security culture of a company refers to the behavior and attitude of the company's personnel towards security. A good security culture reduces security risks and supports a company's competitiveness. Risk prevent is most successful in a company where the management is committed to risk management. In four out of five companies surveyed, the management personally participates in security development. A lack of internal co-operation and co-ordination may also form a significant obstacle to corporate security because potential risks should be examined from the different viewpoints of all areas of operation. A quarter of the responding companies reported do not co-operate with each other when dealing with security issues. Thus, I feel employers need to concern how achieve security development to themselves to reduce loss threats. What are the future focal points for security development? They include: data security, key personnel security, personal security, security of production facilities and equipment, prevention against other threats, preparations to deal with terrorism. Because unknown risks can't be controlled. Before it can prepare for risks, the company must understand the risks that are related to their activities and operating environment, risk assessment helps a company to evaluate the internal and external threats, it may be facing. So, a through assessment that is regularly updated helps to guide risk management work.

Why does employer need to prepare psychological medical records or confidential employment check for any employee job application before who decide to employ any new staffs? This method is pre-employment evaluations method to judge or predict whether the employee has criminal record or possible criminal behavior caused before the employer ensures to choose to employ the staff to enter whose firm to work. For example, the employer can require the mental health professional to conduct pre-employment an forensic evaluations frequently receive requests for release of the job applicant's forensic psychological medical records report. When a routine clinical report is prepared to guide treatment, it is clear that the report should be released of there is an appropriate patient-initiated authorization. Although, these records belong to the patient. But, does an applicant for job or subject (examinee) of a fitness for duty evaluation have a right to a copy of a report commissioned by an employer or lawyer?

There are many types of evaluations that can generally be referred to as forensic or employment evaluations, and each has characteristics that may make release of the report to the examinee unwise of problematic. Additionally, laws and regulations that define rules for disclosure of these reports are often unclear or contrdictory. So, why employers need to concern this issue. For example, a police department refers an employee to a fitness for duty evaluation. The officer has been involved in a series of confrontations in which deadly force was deployed, and the department wants to know whether the officer has psychological problems that predispose him be more aggressive thn necessary. So, as a employer, you need to concern whether the department has sent or has not sent the officer any file containing internal investigations reports of the various incidents, including names of witnesses and their statements to concern the job applicant's individual behavior to judge whether the chance of who has possible to perform criminal or immoral behavior will occur during who are working in any working environment from whose personal behavior's history medical record. So, you will have more accurate to judge whether who is an easy criminal or not easy criminal person to make decision whether you ought to choose to employee whom or not.

As provisions of health information portability and accountability act (HIPAA), 1996, states that even test results belong to patients as part of their history medical records. If include copy righted and trade secret information, such as test manuals is released by the patient's request. But professional ethics and HIPAA regulations don't fully consider the complications of release of information issues in employment and forensic evaluations. Also, the mental health professional can't simply conclude that examinees have a right to them file. However, access of individuals to protected health information, the regulations recognize the right of an individual to access a record set except for the following: 1) psychotherapy notes 2) information compiled in reasonable anticipation of, or for use in a civil, criminal or administrative action or proceeding and 3) when a correctional institution or a covered health care provider may deny access to protect the safety, security, custody, or rehabilitation of other inmates, or the safety of the employee at the institution. Access may also be denied if the information was obtained from someone than a health care provider under a promise of confidentiality and the access would be reasonably likely to reveal the source of the information.

The reasons of internal theft threat occurs in working environment

Why do employees steal? The motivating factors for employee theft are opportunity, rationalization, or need. The removal of any of these factors particularly opportunity will reduce losses. As risk of being caught increases, the probability of theft decreases. When the risk of being caught of low theft may raise. Criminal psychologists indicated that 10% of your employees would not steal from you regardless of the circumstances, 10% will steal at any opportunity and 80% can go either way, waiting to see how serious you are about theft and weighing the risks. Thus, the best defense against internal theft is comprehensive pre-employment screening. A criminal records check and a credit history are a vital part of this process. Because the criminal records check will verify whether an employee has been honest in answering questions about a criminal record. Employers may arrange for a criminal records check by requiring a prospective employee to obtain one as a condition of employment. Also a credit history can reveal whether a person (new staff) is experiencing or has experienced a financial problem. This can help expose a unusual financial need.

How to develop honest behaviors to employees ? Employers must demonstrate to employees that loss prevention is important to them by setting an example. Employers can do this by developing a code of conduct for staff and encouraging communication. To implement proper procedures and policies and ensure compliance to encourage reporting of suspicious circumstances or persons to someone prepared to deal with it, to educate staff on recognition and response to employee theft.

What is burnout? " Staff burnout is defined as a condition of emotional exhaustion, depersonalization and reduced personal accomplishment that can occur among individuals who work with people in some capacity" (Maslach, Jackson & Leiter, 1996, p.4)

How has close relationship between low staff morale and burnout? When economic downturn occurs, the staff size is being reduced, causing longer workdays, fewer opportunities to recharge and relax and greater responsibilities for remaining employees. Ultimately, these changes in the workplace dynamic could cause reductions in staff morale and an increase in burnout in a normally bright and happy workforce. Why does trends/issues of low staff moral and burnout cause? Why does staff burnout behave? Burnout behavior will cause employee attempts to do theft. Who is emotional exhaustion, depersonalization and reduced personal accomplishment. Emotional exhaustion refers to the energy discharge of emotional resources , which is considered the keystone of staff burnout. Staff effects in work environment: higher rates of illness, lower staff moral, increased use of alcohol and drugs, lower creer satisfaction, high staff turnover, reduced quality of service and poor productivity, even more serious criminal internal theft behavior will occur in any workplace.

As unexpected staff burnout is complex problem. Bad emotion factors can cause burnout, include escapism, reflection, long term stressful feeling. So, employers need to concern about how to avid burnout cause. Burnout can cause poor staff morale, such as intrinsic poor motivation, poor organizational commitment and lacking work pride. Why employers need to concern about how to raise staff morale culture because which can notice improved productivity, improved performance and creativity reduced number of days taken for leave, higher attention to detail, safe workplace and n increased quality of work. Otherwise, poor staff moral lack of motivation and interact, decreased working efficiency and could lead to staff's refusal to provide services, even the individual employee who is burn outed who will be influenced to plan to perform criminal theft behaviors to compensate for whose psychology and financial unfair loss from whose employer or colleagues. So, it seems burnout will have chance to cause the employee who is burn outed who choose to do any insider criminal behavior in working environment.

How to predict potential insider threats in working environment

I shall recommend that a behavioral model for predicting potential insider threats in working environment. It is an alarm about employees who pose higher insider threat risks. The insider threat refers to harmful acts that trusted insiders might carry out. For example, something that causes harm to the organization, or an authorized act that benefits the individual. The insider threat is when human behavior depart from established policies, regardless of whether it results from disregard for security policies. The serious types of crimes and threats include terrorism, corruption, bribery etc. as well as the not serious types of crimes and threats include copyright violations, negligent use of classified data, fraud unauthorized ccess to sensitive information and illicit communication with unauthorized recipients in workplace environment. Commonly, it is difficult to predict how the motivation of insiders who commit security fraud. The most of the threats could have been prevented by timely and effective action to address by timely and effective action to address the anger, pain, anxiety, or criminal psychological in cause of risk well in advance of any insider crime.

How can psychosocial behaviors that be predicted increased risk for insider threats? Some criminal psychologist explained insider threat detection, which is based on multiple indicators that not only address work station and network activity logs, but also include preparatory behavior, verbal behavior and personality traits. Instead who recommended consideration of nonclinical instruments that measure personality and behavioral characteristics tests, that not only focus on job suitability and skills, but who don't contain the obvious psychiatric questions, that are easily picked tests indicated any employee selection, but who allow that largely due to the unpredictability of the employees' life and work circumstances in relation to their workplace behavior after being employed. The poor immoral behaviors, such as absenteeism, disciplinary issues and drug alcohol abuse will be caused by an insider risk evaluation when the employee feels whose employer consider whose personal moral behavior considerately. So, it will cause employee's individual negative attitude to be caused if who feels whose employer's dissatisfaction with whose work organization is a powerful predictor of workplace fraud to himself/herself moral behavior in any workplace environment. Thus, it is an substantial relationship between the employee's perception of injustice of the workplace and whose deviant behavior, such as theft, violence.

In the case of an employee trying to gain financially be exploiting a corporation's intellectual property, a desire may be driven by the satisfaction of causing costly damage to the corporation, but it can be also include a motive of financial gain. In either case, the employee may have exhibited stress or some for of dissatisfaction about whose circumstances. These factors, if properly evaluated in a timely manner, could alert an organization about a developing insider crime . Identifying employees who show risk of insider threat has two benefits: preventing an unnecessary cost to the employer, and helping the employee before a bad situation changes worse.

The relationship between workplace monitoring and trust is complex. On the one hand, opponents claim workplace monitoring that an employer's use of monitoring devices, whether convert or overt, threatens both employee privacy and morale. Such as, when the employer feels doubtful to lack of trust whose behavior may contribute to employee job dissatisfaction. Also, some criminal psychologists explain when attitudes are negative about surveillance, employees are less likely to be committed to their work, who will display lower organizational citizenship behaviors. So, it seems employer can not let any individual employee discover that who is doubtful whose attempts to do immoral behavior and to use surveillance to supervise when who is working in any workplace environment daily. Because who will raise whose employees feel unhappy to work in whose workplace environment and to influence who reduce productivity or providing poor customer service performance long term. Hence, employer needs to let whose employees to have more confidence to work in whose workplace environment to avoid staff (leaving) turnover numbers will increase.

How to reduce internal risk and fraud losses in work environment

I shall recommend how to reduce internal risk and fraud losses. Advanced detection techniques, such as behavior profiling, peer analysis, fraud correlation and complex statistical analysis can quickly help identify fraudulent employee activities, mitigating direct financial losses, and non transactional losses, including data theft, regulatory fines and reputational damage. Other methods include: out-of-the box, browser-based investigation capabilities, such as advanced query tools, case and workflow management, and SAR filing combined with integration of various systems, eliminates the manual processes of sifting through the data, automates detection of common employee violations, and supports case-building efforts. Besides identify and discover all content inside your network that represents risk. Effective insider threat management requires an organization to locate and classify its assets and to remain continuously watchful of insider behavior and associated risk. For example, key members of your organization should meet to prioritize critical areas of concern. You could use a simple scoring system, such as 1 to 10, or low, medium and high to assist in your prioritization. Your focus, should center on those assets that receive the highest priority or those that would be most costly to your organizations. This content should include all data and files containing personal or customer information and intellectual property or other sensitive data. Each organization may define these assets and incidents differently as they will vary depending on the industry or focal point of your organization.

What is insider scientific theft? It may include secret documents, company financial data, client's confidential data. Example assets at risk by vertical market include: Banking and credit companies which identifies theft, account skimming, funds, diversion. Financial firms whose mergers and acquisition plans, non-public financial information and private research. Retail organizations whose pricing information, personal information, on credit card holders. Public companies whose earnings information not yet distributed to the market, new product information before release, intellectual property. The government whose national secrets, classified and personal information.

How to reduce insider scientific theft risk? Once identified and prioritized this content should be fingerprinted and inventoried to ensure that it is not sent out via e-mail, instant messaging (IM) or copies to USB or other mobile storage devices. Security risks are not circumvented through simply data-leak prevention, as which are fair detectors of mostly one vector of communications, such as out bound data streams, mostly e-mail. The insider scientific theft, such as typical customer data-loss investigations include that deliberate theft of client lists for profit by employees with access to client data (ID theft); leak of customer data is lost or stolen laptops with client data, However, client data losses are sometimes accidental , e.g. losing a

Laptop containing tens or even more than one thousand customer records, but the data loss that enterprises need to monitor mostly closely are the deliberate acts, such as theft of personal data for resale (ID theft). A laptop can happen to anyone, from a junior salesperson to the CEO. For example, some deliberate client data thefts involve contractors or outsourced service, such as call centers users have little management oversight to the company.

How to predict insider intellectual property theft behavior? Typical intellectual property investigations include that deliberate theft of IP for financial gain, unintentional leak follow up when also open to accidental disclosure, intellectual property, such as CAD files, product plans, proprietary formulas etc. are typically targeted for deliberate theft in a manner that either harms the company for reasons of deliberate press leaks, anonymous sending to competitors etc. or to further the perpetrator's own direct objectives taking IP to a competitor for a new job. Also, company can achieve policies that monitor off-hours activity hundreds of pages printed at 4: 50 AM. Per working day, unusual mobile storage use (gigabyte transfers daily), or suspicions activities with applications (taking a screenshot of a custom CAD design window) are helpful with investigations.

What kind of organizations need to concern intellectual property theft? Hospital, financial institutions are retailers are all highly regulated due to the high volumes of confidential data each organization manages. Banks and financial institutions most protect customer's confidential personally identifiable information. Internally, enterprises need to monitor to corporate governance issues (i.e. employees handbook issues, like harassment that might also put the company at legal risk. Cases involving theft of confidential information include cases in which current or former employees or contractors intentionally exceed or misuse an authorized level of access to networks, systems or data with the intention of stealing confidential information form the organization. Some psychologists had researched to indicate who take insiders were in any organizations. 80% of the insiders who stole confidential information worse and stole over half hold technical positions, 25% were former employees, the other 75% were current employees when who committed whose illicit activity. Interestingly, 45% of the insiders who were current employees at the time of their theft had already accepted positions with another company. Why who do it? Some insiders were financially motivated, for example, stealing information to commit credit card fraud or selling information to their company's competitors. Others were about to start new jobs or form their own companies and felt entitled to the information.

How who did it? More than 75% of the insiders had authorized access when who committed their theft. Only former employee was given authorized access to do some additional work, who used that access to commit whose theft. The rest of the authorized uses were fairly evenly split between privileged and unprivileged users. More than 75% of the insiders used their own usernames and passwords to commit thefts. However, an important factor in dealing with insider threats is understanding the profiles (job, status with company etc.) . Clearly having an idea of user and behavioral profiles can make investigations easier. Thus, an enterprise could have built strong general monitoring policies around its core intellectual property, when deploying more policies around those with constant access to core IP. Additionally the enterprise can work more closely with as human resources department to identify at risk employees and deploy, even more focused policies to those users that specifically look for activities, such as high volume printer output after hours, or large files copies to USB drives or other leading indicators of taking IP out the door to their new job. So, employers could not neglect to concern high technological insider theft behaviors from any organizational key employee's immoral performance in any organizational computer departments.

How to use psychological methods to avoid insider theft loss?

The challenge of fraud directed against a business is increased by the diversify and deceptive nature of those crimes. Deception is a key element of workplace fraud, and a company may realize too late that it has been victimized. An appropriate response to the threat of potential areas that are at risk, recognizing the fraud related threats, and understanding the potential fraud, organization points both internal and external. The criminal mind is ever alert to seeming new and unique ways to separate a business from its assets. In business crime, it can seem white-collar crime, such as fraud, misconduct and related financial threats anti-fraud professionals agree that fraud and misconduct activities involve dishonesty and deception that can drive value to any business, either directly or indirectly to earn benefit. Fraud involves the intent to defraud, it relies on the person's deception to accomplish their fraudulent activity. Some criminal psychological research showed fraud is not accomplished via honest mistake or error. Also fraud can manifest itself in a wide variety of ways and originate from a number of different sources.

What does motive people to commit fraud? Criminologists have identify three elements, that are often form the rationalization, opportunity and pressure. Opportunity refers to the situation and circumstances that make it possible for fraud to occur. For example, an employee with uncontrolled access to company funds has the opportunity to misappropriate those funds. So effective internal controls can reduce or even eliminate opportunities for fraud. Pressure and/ or incentive helps explain why and when fraud occurs. Fraud occurs when fraud pressures or incentives outweigh and overcome, the pressures and incentives to act honestly. Thus, it can become the motivation to act fraudulently. The cause of seasons include lifestyle issues, living beyond one's means; personal debt, e.g. excessive credit and use gambling results, .e.g. poor operating results, desire to avoid business failure, meet requirements of lenders. So, if a company can recognize when and where excessive pressure/ incentives may to present, it can use that information in fraud prevention and may be have detection efforts and take action to avoid business-related pressure/incentives in order to reduce fraud risk. For example, in effective fraud prevention program can increase pressures and incentives to act honestly by emphasizing a perception of detection, underscored by the company's demonstrated, consistent commitment to taking appropriate and certain action once fraud is discovered. Rationalization means to the need for people to somehow justify their fraudulent actions in their own minds. A person involves in a fraud attempts to psychologically accept whose own actions and emotionally. Rationalization are not generally known to others and therefore difficult to detect. In addition, persons with low moral mind may feel little need to rationalize their behavior. In fact, some employee with to those criminal matters in office, e.g. asset misappropriation, fraudulent financial statements and records and corrupt or prohibited practices. White-collar crime includes the company's financial statements , internal and external, books and records of business may be targets for fraud, Such as manipulated to hide fraud , e.g. to prevent discovery of an asset misappropriation and/or falsified to accomplish a fraud, e.g. to cause unjustified financial rewards, such as executive bonuses based on falsified financial performance data. This occurrence is not employee's stealing behaviors, but if one staff, e.g. accountant who has incorrect or fraudulent mind to do wrong financial data presentation to aim to get himself/herself benefits from whose employer. Then, whose immoral behavior is such as carrying on illegal stealing criminal behavior in office.

Modern high technological theft and insider threat often occurs in office, including concerns around intellectual property (IP) theft by employees or outsiders impersonating employees. The increasing incident of IP theft, data and other assets are caused by company insiders. With the rapid transition of every industry to being driven by software, it's not surprising that the impact of cyber-theft has more potential than even serious damage clearly . Clearly leakage of IP has consequences damaging competitiveness, innovation and potentially leading to massive commercial losses. For example, computer games industry, if its new launch was stolen by an insider computer department employee or programmer, who is already to leave the company. Or being an automotive firm that is just found out that is top secret code associated with a new breakthrough in vehicle engineering, other side of the world, simply because someone managed a valid employee's ID to steal the new vehicle engineering invention to sell to competitors. Other example, organized criminal groups' frequently use the intent to commit fraudulent actions in the banking and financial system and the underground marketplace where cyber-criminals can buy and sell stolen information and identities to earn illegal money.

How to avoid company's secret data loss or theft from insider? Employees who move data to insecure locations in order to ease their work processes create risk by exposing the data to external hackers or bad actors who work within a company at supply chain partner companies or among contractors. Besides, employees leaving are taking sensitive data with them is a problem. This includes not only trade secrets related to the programs with which on close employees were involved. In many quick action incidents, attackers will access data who have rarely on never accessed, execute events that change data and finally move large amounts of removable data to storage devices, personal machines or public cloud storage. So, employers also need to concern computer department any employee individual secret data theft behavior to avoid intelligence asset loss.

In addition of white collar labor crime, non white-collar or blue labor crime also include armed robberies offer a great opportunity for injury or death, current and former employees and their friends are often involved, the most of common times for an armed robbery are during opening and closing periods. So, cash in the restaurant should be kept to a mini8mum and anyone either hourly employee or manager , none of employees will be allowed to be alone in the restaurant and employees should enter and leave utilizing the safe security system to reduce any lose in restaurant any environment. For hospitality industry, it also often occurs stolen matters, credit card stolen behavior is popular in hotels. Because some hotel accept clients to choose to use credit card to pay hotel rent commonly. Another concerning trend, not only attentions to the hospitality industry, when once used to be primarily a guest services issue has now grow into a big financial problem. With the adoption of the new payment card industry security standards, hotel will not being compliance with these security standards risk processing fee surcharges that can amount to thousands of dollars in additional expenses. In order to reduce the occurrence of theft of credit card data, I shall recommend methods, such as precious guest folios with credit card information should be placed in secure offsite storage, 30 days after an event. Never put guest credit card information on internal documents; swiping the credit card will transfer the required data to the property management system , displaying the last four digits of the credit card number is adequate for all routine transactions. One of the main reasons for a chargeback is fraud, it is important to monitor chargebacks and the reason codes, and implement procedures to reduce the number of chargebacks occurring, store all guest credit card data in one secure location. This site be monitored be closed circuit television system and have an electronic lack to provide an audit trail, use fax programs that can only be assessed via secure password protected computer; restrict access to guest data to a limited number of trusted employers will help to reduce employee theft of this information.

So, I feel how to create a positive work environment which is needed. This encourages employees to follow the best interests of the business. Fair employment practice, written job description, clear organizational structure, comprehensive policies and procedures, span lines of communication between management and employees and positive employee recognition will help to reduce the likelihood of internal fraud and theft. For pharmaceutical industry, it also has insider theft occurrence. I recommend to use video surveillance to implement an expanded two-person rule, recording attention to security, and establishing incident databases and experience to supervise staffs behaviors. All situations involving protection against potential insider threats involve some combination of managing the potential insiders and managing the items to be protected which might to thing, that might be stolen, areas of a facility that might be targeted, people who might be stolen, damaged or misused. Most high security organizations perform some form of background check before giving people access to items, areas or information to be protected or information about how these are secured. The thoroughness of such checks varies widely, ranging from a simple criminal background check (or less) to a full investigation, in which the person's career, health to detect notable changes in behavior or circumstances that may bear on their inappropriate behaviors noticed by environments. For example, insiders must undergo new background every few years to maintain their clearance and staff are encouraged to report any changes in their own circumstances. Both initial background screening and ongoing monitoring of employee behavior raise issues of privacy and civil liberties. Also keeping up staff moral and motivation and convincing them to active participants elements of an effective program to protect against insiders. One obvious step is ensuring that staff are adequately paid, so that anger at the organization for undervaluing, they don't add to the motivation contributing factor. At the moments, the organization's ability is offer incentives and disincentives is much demanded and the employee's loyalty to the organization's may be minimal. For example, no one would be allowed if no legal arrangement to enter restricted drug (pharmaceutical) store. It can reduce drug theft chance occurrence in drug store easily.

An insider threat is generally defined as a current or former employee, contractor or other business partner who has on had authorized access to an organization's network system or data and intentionally misused that access to negatively affect the confidentiality, or availability of the organization's information or information systems. Insider threats to include theft, fraud and competitive advantage are often carried out through abusing access rights, theft or materials and mishandling physical devices. Insiders don't always act alone and may not be aware they are aiding a threat actor (i.e. the unintentional insider threat). It is important that organizations understand normal employee baseline behaviors and also ensure employees understand how who may be used as an theft insider. Because prediction to who will be insider, it will reduce loss of risk to any organizations. How to deter the theft insider behavioral threat? Building a baseline understanding of the personalities and behavioral norms of those previously defined as an theft insiders will detecting their immoral easier. However, some general behavioral characteristics of theft insiders at risk of becoming a threat include: introversion, financial need, destructive behavior, passive aggressive, ethical flexibility, reduced loyalty, self image, minimizing their mistakes or faults, inability to assume responsibility for their actions intolerance of criticism, self-perceived value exceeds performance lack of empathy, immoral behavior towards law enforcement, pattern of frustration and disappointment, history of managing crises ineffectively.

These are psychological characteristics of personal insider at risk of becoming a threat to any within organizational businesses‘ departments. Individuals that exhibit these characteristics may reach a point at which who carry out immoral activity against the organization. One of the best prevention measures is to train employees to recognize and report behavioral indicators exhibited by peers or business partners. Some behavioral indicators of threat activity include: remotely access the network when on vacation, sick time, works odd hours without authorization; notable enthusiasm for overtime weekend or unusual work schedules; unnecessary copies material especially, it it is proprietary or classified; interest in matters outside of the scope of their duties; signs of ability, such as drug or alcohol abuse, financial difficulties, gambling activities, poor mental health behavior. So wen behavioral characteristics, who ought concern how whose personal performance or behavior in office or workplace environment considerately.

Based on above warning signs among employees, such as expected wealth, unusual foreign travel, irregular work hours or unexpected absences. Identifying behavioral indicators may be difficult, particularly if who don't occur for a long period of time and therefore don't set a pattern. Therefore a good understanding of risk characteristics and events that may predict those characteristics is essential . However, individuals cause threats for a variety of reasons; some theories are considered by criminal psychologists such as: general deterrence theory, it indicates that person commits crime if expected benefit outweighs cost of action; social learning theory, it indicates the person commits crime of associates with peers. Theoy of planned behavior indicates the person's intention (attitude subjective norms and perceived behavior control) towards crime key factors in predicting behavior; situational crime prevention theory indicates crime occurs when both motive and opportunity exist. These behaviors and indicators whether detected via technology or human observance techniques are intended to detect the insider. It is equally important though to create productive and healthy work environments to help to reduce the unintentional insider threat. Some countermeasures include training employees to recognize social media threat vectors; training continuously to maintain the proper levels of knowledge of knowledge skills and abilities, conducting training and improve awareness of risk perception and cognitive biases that affect decision making, improving use ability of security tools and software to reduce the likelihood of system induced human error, enhancing awareness of the unintentional insider threat; providing effective security practices , e.g. two factors authentication for access; maintaining staff values and attitudes that co-operate with organizational mission and ethics.

Nowadays, some security technologies can detect/ prevent insider attacks, such as: data/file encryption, data access monitoring ; SIEM or other log analysis; data loss prevention, data redaction; enterprise identity and access management, data access control, detection/prevention systems and enterprise digital rights management solution etc. technology insiders detection systems. Besides, some deterrence methods include: deploy data centers, not system, centric security, crowd source security, use positive social engineering, thinking a marketer to build a baseline on volume , frequency and amount based on hourly, weekly and monthly normal patterns, using centralized logging to detect data near insider termination, requiring identification for an assets, e.g. access cards, password, inventory check out, frequent visits to sites may indicate how productivity job and potential habit, announce the use of policies that monitor events like unusual networks traffic spikes, volume at USB/mobile storage use, volume of off hour printing activities and inappropriate use of encryption; implement employee recognition programs that offer public praise to insider threat motivated; provide avenues for employees to vent concerns and frustrations to insider threat motivated; authorize users based on access and conduct periodic audits to detect inappropriately granted access or access that exists from previous job functions and should be removed.

Finally, I feel continual training is always a recommended option. For example, free of charge courses that organizations may want to consider offering to employees, contractors, and others that meet the description of an "insider". Training ought concentrate on teaching how to protect your organizations teaching how to protect your organizations information and systems from unauthorized insider misuse for technology criminal insiders. Otherwise, employers need to provide psychological criminal training to teach how to predict whose staff individual behavior to avoid any staff who do theft behavior before any staff's immoral behavior will be caused in whose working place environment.

To conclude, business crimes are very popular. However, technological theft insiders or non technological theft insiders both are the same important factors to influence any business development for long term successfully. Thus, employers ought need to concern employees' immoral behaviors to avoid high risk loss in office, factory, shop or any workplace environment.

Essentials of organizational behavioral learning

The importance of management skills is essential, if any organizations hope to raise efficiency or improve performance. Organizations need to learn how to balance hard and soft skill, how to manage social and human skills whch reflect the ability to get along with other people are increasingly important attributes at all levels of management.

Managers ought need to spend most time operating between the " hard skills" , such as conducting disciplinary matters or how to allocate of budgets, and " soft skills" , such as counselling, or giving support and advice to a member of staff. Managers also needed to be trained to raise technical competence, related to specific tasks, how to supervise and train subordinate staffs, and with day-to-day subordinate staff, and with day-to-day operations concerned in the actual production of goods and services; social and human skills relates to interpesonal relationship in working with and through other people, and how to judge to achieve effective teamwork and direction, and leadership of staff to achieve co-ordinated effort to particular situation and flexibilty in adopting the most appropriate style of management, raising conceptual ability in order to view he complexities of the operations of the organization as a whole, including environmental influences.

Mc Donald soft skill organizational behavior

It also involves decision-making skills, relates to the overall making of the organization and to its stragegic planning in long time, such as McDonald restaurant has good strategic management to manage its global branches of franchise restaurants in organizational behavioral view successfully. So, it can attract many investors buy its franchises to learn how to do McDonald fast food restsurants . It's investors number is increasing, due to it has good significant organizational behavior as well as its managers know how to apply " soft skills" and " hard skills" to manage them effectively.

So, organizational behavior and organizational performance seems have close relationship. If the organization can build the most effective and efficient organizational behavior, managers know how to manage employee individual behavior, then the performance ought will be improved , even customers won't complaint or feel unsatisfactory easily, they will feel satisfactory to their staffs service performance, such as McDonald fast food restaurant case, global McDonald fast food franchise restaurants eating customers complain bumber is low in general, because instead of their front line service staffs performance and attitude can let them to feel satisfactory,

The most influential soft skill to bring its fast food eating customers feel satisfactory or they are persuaded to choose its sale service to replace other similar fast food restaurants sale service. The reason is because that , when they buy its fast food, or soft drink, they must be arranged to give one number ticket. So, they do not need to spend long time to queue in any McDonald fast food restaurants, they can leave McDonald restaurant to go to other places and they wont' worry that McDonald staffs forget to make their fast food or soft drink when they leave. Because they can give the number ticket to indicate their number to the staff to take their fast food or soft drink any time. For example, if the eating customer's ticket number is 30, and the screen indicates next number future cooking is 10, then he will feel that he can leave McDonald to spend about 15 minutes to come back. Even, if his coming back time is exceed 15 minutes, and the screen indicates number is 40. Although, he is late, but he may ask the staff to take his fast food or soft drink immediately. So, he does not need to worry about that he can take his fast food or soft drink even he is late to come back. So they avoid to queue long time in McDonald, they can come back after half hour, even after one hour. When they come back, they only need to give their number ticket to confirm that the had paid money to buy fast food or soft drink. When the front line staff see that number from their ticket. They will go to kitchen to take their prepared fast food or soft drink to give them immediately. it is one effective time management " soft skill" to avoid eating customers feel angry or bad emotion when they need to queue in long time in any one Mc Donald restaurant. They can choose to leave Mcdonald restaurants any long time. It is one efficient and effective 2 soft skill customer service management skill in any one nowadays McDonald front line . So , it's success depends on its front line staff " don't need eating people to queue long time" in any one McDonald restaurant.

Convenient framework of analysis of organizational behavior

Any organizations ought need have a convenient framework of analysis if they hope to manage their organizational behavior efficiently. I shall explain what a convenient framework of organizational behavior analysis means as below:

The top level is what nature and purpose of the

organization, then next middle level concerns learning how to manage " behavior of people", " process of management", " organizational context" , next is middle level learning how to adapt any environment influences. The final process to any organizations. They hope to achieve improving organizational performance in success as well as organizational processes as well as how to execution of work to the most success.

It is one important service soft skill method to let global McDonald restaurants can continue to attract many eating people to choose to but their fast food or soft drink , instead of reduced price or coupon sale method in global fast food restaurant market. So, its success depends on how to mix of the practical and the soft skill service performance strategy to eating customer long time queue bad emotion theoretical psychological strategy, it must be linked to a single aim, such as Mc Donald has its single aim to front line staffs, is that how to avoid eating people need to stay in McDonald restaurant to queue long time to let them to feel angry and unsatisfactory to its global any McDonald franchise restaurants. So it comfirms that , many its global eating people don't like to queue and to stay in McDonald long time, when the Ms Donald has many people are staying in McDonald in busy time.

Thus, in organizational behavioral view, they will be persuaded to choose to buy MsDonald fast food in perference, because its unique service feature, when other fast food restaurants can not implement this front lines do not need queue method in their fast food restaurants. It implies that effective front line service skill may be one important factor to influence any clients' choices in preference.

How to apply hard skill and soft skill to solve inefficient problem?

The theme of inefficiency will experience to any organizations, if they lack effective organizational behavioral management strategy. It assumed that workers who were not good at one particualr task, would be best at some other tasks in any teams. There is however, no certainty of this in practice. It concerns workers from an engineering view point and as machines , but the one best way of performing a task is not always the best method for every worker. So, the reduction of physical movement to find the one best way is or always beneficial and some " wasteful" movements are essential to the overall rhythm of work.

So, if the organization hopes to achieve effective organizational behavior, the organization needs to concern these soft skill and hard skill issues they may include:

1. High wages from increased output.
2. The removal of physical strain from doing works the wrong way.
3. Development of the workers and the opportunity for them to undertake tasks , they were capable of doing and
4. Elimination of the " boss" and the duty of management to help workers.

For example on factory raising efficient organizational behavior aspect, the factory may implement these soft skill and hard skill both strategies, such as: To assist the stores in better customer service by having the merchandise ready to go on the floor, saving space in the stockroom, and creating customer goodwill, to increase the units per hour produced, to performance the job duties as efficiency and effectively as possible, avoiding bureaucracies organization, it emphasised the importance of administration based on experise (rules of experts) and administration based on discipline (rules of officials). Because one when burea staffs are working in one serious or strict bureaucracies organization, they will feel not happy and unsatisfactory to their manager behavior. So, managers' soft management skill ought often need to revise when need to be changed to be better or improve their performance, such as:

The tasks of the organization are allocated as official duties among the various positions, there is an implied clear -out division of labor and a high level of specialisation, a hierarchical authority applies to the organization of offices and positions, uniformity of decisions and actions is achieved through formally established systems, of rules and regulations. Together work a structure of authority , this enables the coordination of various activities within the organization, an imperaonal orietnation is expected from officials in their dealings with clients and other officials. This is designed to result in rational judgments by officials in the performance of their duties as well as employment by the organization is based on technical qualifications and constitues a lifelong career for the officials, e.g. how to apply specialisation more to the job than to the person undertaking the job.

This makes for continuity because the job usually continues of the present job holder leaves, hierarchy of authority it makes for a sharp distination between administrators and the administered or between management and workers, within the management ranks these are clearly defined levels of authority, system of rules aims to provide for an officials and impersonal operaton, sules are generally stable although some rules may be changed as modified with impersonality means that how allocation and exercise authority should not be complex.

Reference

Maslach, C., Jackson, S.E. & Leite,M.P. (1996). Maslach Burnout inventory manual (3 rd ed.) Palo Alto, CA: Consulting psychologists Press

FOUR

Organizational Crime Psychology Causes

In general, psychology science is often mislead to explain what its functions wrongly by our society. Psychology English is come from " psyche" and " logos" two words consist. The prior word means " soul" and the later word means " theory" . So, psychological science is explanation of mind science. It is one kind of research human mind activities science or it is one kind of research human's behavioral science. Any kinds of human's Behaviors mean observation from environment influences. But, nowadays, psychological science of new explanation means human's mind and behavior observation both aspects research.

So, what does psychological science mean? In fact, anyone can be one part time (folk psychologist) . For example, any one child can own ability or knows how to predict any one's psychology or mind successfully, e.g. he knows how to keep his toy in not easy discovered or secret location in his house or school or any places, and he aims to make wrong direction to mislead his friends need to spend much time to find his toy. He aims to achieve none any his friends or patents can find or discover this toy easily consequently. It explains that any one adult , even child, he does not need to be taught, but he can have himself mind or ability to feel whether he ought need to how to do himself behavior to achieve his aim immediately. This kind of personal creative or own protective behavior or mind research that is psychologists want to find any answers to support and to explain why and how child can own this kind of psychological mind. It is one part of psychological research aim.

Why does psychologists know what you want easily or they can make more accurate judgement? In general, psychologists feel need to do any psychological science research aims, because they want to discover or find what are the thinking or mind about any one in order to make the absolute accurate judgement. Psychologists' duties need to research any one's psychological activities, why he/she feel happy or sad or satisfactory or any emotion, which factors influence he/she Has this kind of emotion and what the relationship is between of them. For example, the person assumes that he often feels difficult to sleep, he will attempt to buy any useful drugs or medicines to eat to help him to sleep easily. But, if he can not still feel that any kinds of drug can help him to feel enough sleeping after he eats it easily. Then, he has possible to find one psychologist to help him to find what factors cause him to feel difficult to sleep. SO, finding any factors to cause any one feels disappoint or failure or fear or difficult to do any thing etc. different negative emotion challenges, it may be any psychologist's duty to know how to find the main factor(s) to help to serve his patients satisfactorily.

Some people feel psychologists' duties are easy. It is wrong view point. In fact, they need spend long time to research any psychological topics and they are very difficult to research in order to conclude any results or answers.

I shall indicate both interesting cases , they concern how psychologists can help their patients successfully as below:

For bind people example, some bind or without enough eye sight seeing any thing people who can not see any thing long time, some psychologists can help them to see any things clearly when they are old age successfully in possible.

For another horse lotto win money participates case, there is one group people decides to invest money to participate this time horse lotto winning money competition. Before, every time horse competition, they share their opinions to concern every time horse lotto competition. And then, they will concentrate nervous to discuss and make group participation final decision to choose which numbers of horses, they decide to buy together. For every horse lotto competition, it has these three kinds of different level of decisions. The first kind is the least risk and prudential decision, it is without any investment money is needed to buy any hour number in the horse lotto competition. The another more risk decision is invested less money to some horses , they feel that they have possible to race in win and the final is the most risk decision is that to invest less money to some horses only, but they do not know that they have no possible to win money in the time horse lotto race competition with every participant personal average opinion comparison.

So, the participant's overall final decision may include three results: (1) more prudential decision result, (2) more risk decision result (3) without more prudential and more risk decision result.

So, psychologists can attempt to help them to apply psychological concept and theory to give recommendation how to raise chance to win this horse race lotto competition before he had gathered any horse past race experience and winning or lose times information to analyze every horse's winning chance rate. However, the psychologist must not guarantee they can win any horse race lotto in this competition. He can only give suggestion to help them to make more accurate judgement whether they ought choose which number of horse to buy.

What investigation methods as used by psychological science? For example, researching about how much violence level to the movie, you need to do surveys to enquire any participants whose feeling to this violence movie. Your investigating method is survey method. For another example, your participation to research the patients eat the drug how to influence their feeling or emotion, it is drug laboratory experiment method. For final example, you participate the activity and the psychologists use video camera to record your behavior, it is one observation method.

Some psychologists apply experiment psychological method to find what the main factors influence the student feels bore or difficult to learn anything. Some psychologists apply physical psychological method to find what factors cause close relationship between building biology process (stage) and human behaviors, e.g. How do our brains carry on analyzing our daily activities? Where are our brain part locations for our emotion, activity and mind leading functions? Has it same brain activity to learn between reading English and reading Chinese language? Some psychologists apply development psychological method to research how and why human's character causes and personal psychological mind development process, social behavioral development. Hence, psychological science research may be our whole person life development process research. From student stage, we have chance to encounter learning difficulties, when working age stage, we may encounter challenge how to cooperate to work with team members efficiently in any organizations, till to our old age stage, we may encounter our psychological and mental and physical health challenge. Hence, psychologists need to apply their professional psychological knowledge to help us to solve our any personal challenges , when we have chance to encounter in our different life stages

Do you feel that your behaviors will be influenced by non-control or unknown factors influence? Do you ensure that your behaviors are careless causes? Psychological analysis function can be applied to these aspect: It can help us to know what myself actual ability owning to do any matters. For example, because we feel happy, so we will feel that we have this kind of ability to do this matter, even it is difficult to let us to feel to finish. Because happy feeling motivate us to attempt to do this matter, but it does not represent that we must own this kind of effort to succeed to finish this matter. It is only ourselves personal ability feeling or we have no own this kind of ability in fact. Otherwise, actual myself ability is between myself ability and exceeding myself super ability; actual myself ability represents logic and clever or talent that you own, they you're your protective ability. We can follow actual principles to choose to attempt to do any matters in order to achieve satisfactory feeling.

So, when we know what is actual ourselves abilities own, we will have more chance to finish the matter successfully. Because we have known whether what our actual abilities own to do the matter to achieve more successful chance. The final psychological mind analysis is that when we know what our social principle is and our life aim or goal or intention is, then we won't limit out actual owning abilities to attempt to achieve our any life aims or goals successfully in the end our life.

For example, some talent scientists, talent musicians, talent actors. They had known what their actual abilities in their life own. SO, they can have more confidence to attempt to do " exceeding themselves abilities behaviors" to achieve their life goals successfully. They have these personal characteristics: They had correct or right psychological mind analysis to know whether what they real need or hope to achieve as well as what their actual themselves " super owning abilities" that they ensure to own in order to accept to spend long time to learn how to raise their unique skills or techniques as well as doing owning super ability behaviors to achieve their life dreams. For some space scientists, actors, super sport people their abilities are seemed to own god helping, their super abilities are due to they had known whether what their unique owning abilities are different to general humans. So, psychological mind analysis function aims to let any people attempt to find or discover whether they have any unique abilities , they are unknown and psychologists need to help them to attempt to find any unique abilities in order to create their talent skills or techniques in possible.

What is organizational crime behavioral mind?

In general, in our living environment, we attempt to apply basic learning principle to change our behaviors. It is very common situation. We can observe someone's behaviors in order to learn their skills. For learning basket ball , football playing sport skills example, the basket ball , football players must not need the basket ball, football coach leaders to teach them how to play. They can observe any one football or basket ball team players to learn how their skills to play in proficient very easily. They only need to spend long time to observe their skills in order to learn their skills in success. It is observation learning method, though these observations in order to learning their abilities in success. It is one interesting topic to psychologists' research concerns whether we can observe any person's skills or techniques in order to learn their same level skills or techniques in success.

The question is that whether observation is right or wrong learning behavior or method to any leaners. It is general psychologists have interest to research topic. In general, they believe that our behaviors can be caused by external and internal both factors. The potential environment seems to everyone to be same, but actual environment is ourselves behaviors how are created. For example, one meeting environment people treat themselves attitudes are the same, but one person behaves more rude and not polite and causes noise feeling in whole meeting environment, so his not polite behavior influences the meeting environment people treat him more punishment, but less appreciation. Otherwise, any other people perform their

same behaviors , such as polite and quite personal attitude in the meeting environment. So , many people can create more appreciation, but less punishment behaviors between them in whole meeting environment. It means that we can create chance to ourselves in different environment. It depends on whether how we perform our behavior and feeling to adapt the different environment needs. Such as this meeting environment, when many people perform their behaviors to like to listen other people what they are speaking in quiet personal attitude and they are polite to let any one speak to express his/her opinion in prior in the whole meeting environment. So, these kind of personal behavioral performance attitude is accpeted to whole members. Otherwise, the only one member, he often performs himself behaviors to argue and rude attitude and he also performs not like to listen any one personal opinion, he only

believe his opinion must be the best among all of these members in whole meeting. So, he won't be appreciated his opinion performance and he will have punishment feeling from other members as well as he often feels arguement and he needs to spend much time to argue and support his opinions to other members' opposite opinions

in whole meeting process. Hence, in general any environment, we will be influenced to decide whether we ought choose to do ourselves behaviors in order to satisfy others people's acceptance more easily. Such as this meeting environment example, when some members feel their behaviors are appreciated or accepted , due to their performance and attitude are polite , liking acceptance to listen other opinions, without causing noise and argument, without performing perosnal attitude to let other feel himself/herself opinion must the best among all memebers. In this meeting members' discussion time, this kind of polite and liking listening, liking acceptance other opinions personal attitude behavior will be appreciated. So, many

memebers will feel to be appreciated among of them. Otherwise, the one member often perform rude and not polite personal attitude, and he only
likes others listen his opinion before anyone. He only feel that his opinion must be the best among of all members. However, he does not like to change his attitude to accept to listen other opinions before, he likes to cause arguement to discuss their opinions among of them and his behavior will let many members to feel rude. Due to he does not like accept to change his behavior in whole meeting environment. SO, he must feeling to be punished and without any appreciation in whole meeting
environment.

Hence, our behaviors ought be controlled or dominated by extrenal environment more than ourselves mind control if we hope our behaviors are accepted by many people in society in general. For example, if many the school class students hope to exam to pass this time examination more easily. Their mind will tell them that they will fail the time examination more easily, if they can not spend much time, e.g. one day spends at least 5 to 10 hours maximum per day and three months at least studying period to study hardly at home or school library. Then this class may have more than 50 percent students number will like to attempt to spend at least 5 hours hard to spend study in this three months studying period before this examination in order to achieve passing this examination successful aim or goal or intention.

So, this class student themselves mind is dominated by this classroom learning environment factor influence to persuade their hard studying learning
behavior. However, some lazy students will choose their mind more than learning environment acceptance, so they

will still choose to spend less than 5 hours per day and it is only one month or two month studying period to carry on studying to follow their learning time table daily. Because they
do not feel that they will have high chance to pass this examination if they can spend longer time and longer learning period to gather any
information or teaching material from their school library as well as reducing leisure time and increasing studying time at home before this examination.
So, it explains that somethimes we need to choose to accept to follow to do any decision from either ourselves mind or our external environment as well as we also need to make judgement whether what factor will bring more benefit to us after we choose to do our final decision from either ourselves mind or our external environment factor influence. Because we do not know that whether ourselves mind or acceptance general external environment public mind which can help us to achieve our any goals more easily. So, it explains that why sometimes we needs to do psychological mind analysis between acceptance to ourselves mind more or acceptance to general public mind more in order to implement or
achieve some decisions more success consequently.

IN conclusion, on psychologists psychological mind analysis view points, they need to help patients to know how and why whether they ought follow external environment public mind more
or themsleves mind more in order to judge whether their patients' choice to be decided to do same matters whether it is right or wrong judgement, when their patients feel difficult
to do some decisions and they need their recommendation

to indicate their psychological mind anlaysis assistance need in order to achieve their any decisions more success. So, psychological mind analysis function aims to help patients to know or find reasons tro explain that why they ought choose to do the kind of behaviors and help them to judge whether their behaviors choice or decision is right or wrong to be accepted to general society, even themselves.

Psychologist social service kinds of assistance

In our society, we have many different kinds of psychologists, e.g. criminal psychology, child , young, old age psychology, education psychology,
adult psychology, patient psychology, mental psychology, adult psychology, mental psychology, employee organizational psychology etc. However,
different psychologists will have themselves different psychological service to satisfy their patient mental health needs. In this chapter, I shall
introduce these different kinds of psychologists' tasks how to satisfy their patients' mental health needs. I shall indicate these different kinds
of psychologists' tasks how to satisfy their patients' mental health psychological needs. I also indicate some cases to explain what their tasks differences are.

Firstly, in psychology at work or organizational behavior or employee employee psychological research aspect, it concerns a large part of how people define who they are is by what they do. Work can be a key part of our social identity to build employees sense of themselves. IN special, employees organizational psychology helpe organizations to solve employees mental health and how to bring a good job satisfactory feeling and it can promote psychological wellbeing when people are employed have lower rates of psychological health problems group target.

In psychology at work research aspect, it includes these organizational psychological assistance aspect: How to create a psychological healthy workplace to a meaningful work and what can keep people fulfilled and productive in their jobs ? It considers how to let employees to feel how to do work more attrative, rather than how to make unemployment less attractive. As well as how improving on physical health and sickness absence to some lazy employees' negative mind psychological influence, how the organizational

psychological health of the workforce impacts on organizational health of the organizational performance, how to help organizations measure optimal levels of engagement at work

have significant benefits for the employee. Such higher levels of engagement are characterised by increased levels of angry, dedication, being strongly involved in one's work, experienccing a sense of significance, and being absorbed in one's work so time passes quickly.

So, how to designing work to encourage engagement is also needed to bring beneficial to the employers, helping organizations to attempt to find whether what of a number of key factors influence employees' psychological health and wellbeing in the workplace as well as seeking why and how some individual factors are other are linked to the work environment, e.g. finding what the main reason(s) whether it is/ they are the job insecurity or dissatisfaction or increased risk of low engagement or poor rewarded or long working hours time or feeling boreing etc. different factors influence a decreased productivity to bring a negative impact on the organization's employees.

Hence, employee organizational psychologists need to give their professional opinions to serve any organzations to help them to find what the main factor(s) influence(s) some or all employees' productive performance is(are) caused poor suddenly as well as finding the effective solutions or methods to attempt to help the organizations to recover or improve or raise their employees' productive performance effectively and efficiently in order to achieve the consequence to let all employees will feel happy or feel satisfactory to work in the organizations to avoid employees leaving turnover number increasing occurrence in possible.

Secondly, in concerning mental health and distress preventive psychology aspect, mental health psychologists need to let feeling mental distress hospital patients feel their mental disease or mental pressure can be changed to be health in possible. They need to help any mental patients to find what factors cause their mental sickness (illness), e.g. their mental sicknesses are caused from job stress or personal negative emotion, focus on distress or prior personal sad or unhappy past life experience. THeir mental health service aims to help their mental patients to solve any mental health problems are either illnesses or diseases. All these mental illnesses are assumed by a focus on distress as something
that is perhaps " in the mind". So, all mental illness patients , their mental illnesses are assumes to have cause and effect relationship to their " poor mind" illnesses.

SO, mental health psychologists will focus on their mind research to find why and how they have any mental illnesses suddenly. The term mental illness, for example, any mental health psychologists will suggest that their walk will be illness, and it has a medical character, but that ill will also take a mentalistic or psychological focus. It is the different between a mental health psychologist and a nervous illness doctor how they view their mental illness patients, e.g. a nervous illness doctor will suggest the right medicine (drug) to attempt to help the mental illness patient, but a mental health psychologist will apply psychological knowledge to attempt to help the mental illness patient to solve his mental problems. So, the mental health psychologist will feel psychological health treatment is more useful to compare medicine oe drug eating treamtment, and they will assume that the mental patient's problems is caused due to his psychological emotion factor more than his physical illness factor. For example, one person feels distress or mental pressure, mental health psychologist will feel his distress may be caused from overload job pressure, but a vervous illness doctor will feel his pressure is caused by body physical illness factor more than poor or negative emotion influencing factor. So, one mental health psychologist is one mental health psychologist doctor to find whether what external environment or his/her personal psychological emotion is his main factor to cause his patient feels unpleasant or emotion pressure feeling suddenly in order to solve his psychological illness problem successfully.

Hence, medical psychologists are well aware of the close link between physical disease and mental health. Frequently, psychologists are asked to see a patient who has been admitted to a general medical facility , due to a medical illness or disease that may have a psychological overlay. When providing clinical services to a medical patient in a general hospital, psychologists are finding that they are part of an interdisciplinary team. IN conclusion, any hospitals or clinics must nee medical psychologists give medical psychological methods to solve patients' psychological challenges when he/she feels disappointed or fear himself or herself will die in possible in order to avoid he/she commits suicide easily. Hence, medical psychologist needs to help any patients to build positive emotion continue alive independence. Their role needs to assist doctors to solve their patients' psychological health needs when they are living in hospitals, even they leave their hospitals in future one day.

Thirdly, for crininal psychology social function aspect, why does our society need criminal psychologists? IN our legal system of our society , it is a reflection of what is considered tolerable and intolerable behavior within that particular society, i.e. intolerable behavior is disapproved of by the majority. However, we must have people to anti-social behavior to let our sosciety to know their dissatisfaction, it is their criminal intent major factor. IN fact, any legally wrong or immoral behavior , e.g. burglary, fraud , killing theft, trespass, fighting are caused by the criminal people's negative psychological factor. In general, although many of them had known that they will be punished if they still do criminal behaviors in our society. But, they can not dominate or control themselves to do any criminal behaviors. So, it explains why that we still need criminal psychologists to help them to find why they do criminal behavioral reasons after they had done criminal behaviors as well as they are punished to go to court to be judged consequently.

Criminal psychologists aim to let their criminal patients to know their errors and use professional acriminal psychological methods to help them to learn how to avoid to do any criminal behaviors again after they are free to go to society to prepare to find new jobs to do or beginning re-new life again. The criminal psychologists will make a number of assumptions that any criminal people who have these similar characteristics. They may include as below:

The first assumption is that every individual's behaviors is due to their own interpretation of reality and real environment can influence how any why the person does criminal behavior in society.The second assuption is that people will learn meaning by observing how other people react in society , both positively and negatively. SO , if the person often contact his friends who often react

negative social behavior, they will influence or persuade him to trend to do any criminal behavior more easily in society. The third assumption is that we evaluate our own behaviors according to the meanings, we have learned and that we have acquired from others. So, we will learn any one's behavior and we will make evaluation whether we ought or ought not follow their behaviors

to do. For example, any one knows killing another person is a criminal act. However, in some suitations, for instance, when a peson kills in self-defence, when a legitimate killing because he needs to protect himself body to be attacked to cause hurt, even death as well as he feels that he has possible to be killed if he does not decide to kill the person in the environment immediately. So, criminal psychologists needs to help the killer to feel that he is not a actual killer in psychological view point, although he had killed the person in legal view point in orde to avoid that he commits suicide himself easily in any time.

Hence, any one criminal psychologist, he/she had learnt these criminal psychological knowledge to prepare how to help his / her owning criminal mind and doing criminal behavioral patients to solve negative psychological or negative emotion challenge after they had done criminal activites. Their criminal psychological knowledge may include these several aspects: Knowledge of key concepts and psychological models of criminal behavior, capacity to identify the different perspective on human nature under the theoretical

development and research of any criminal behavioral causes, familiarity with research methodologies commonly employed in the field of criminal psychology, as well as a capacity for analyzing their strengths and weaknesses , a biosocial fame of reference included, ability to examine critically specific offences and apply psychological models of criminality to case studies, awareness of the different prevention, treatment strategies for working with offenders, a range of presentation skills. They need to do face to face contact to spend some time, e.g. one day one to two hours, five days within every week time to talk to the criminal person is prison in order to find whether whar his/her negative psychological or negative emotion factor(s) can cause or influence his/her decision to make any kinds of criminal activities consequently as well as finding the methods to let they feel positive emotion or positive psychological reflection to avoid to do any similar criminal activities again after he/she leave the prision in orde to protect our

social safety, due to their criminal activities occurrence again and reducing criminal rate raising occurrence easily in our society .

Forthly, I will explain what the education psychological function is. Education psychologists may give recommendation to teachers how to encourage their students to themselves learning interest to be raised by their teachers' teaching methods influence or themselves

psychological learning method influence both as well as how to improve their school classrooms teaching -learning environment in order to influence their students feel happy to learn in their classrooms to achieve aim to help them to get high grade results consequently. It is helpful in instructional strategies and provides basis for the selection of appropriate methods, techniques, approaches , tools to satisfy
and fulfil the need of learners that results in better learning, with the help of educational psychological teacher is able to create positive learning environment in the clasrooms resulting in effective learning. So, the educational psychologist plays an important role in making learning easy, joyful and interesting process. Likewise also conflict classroom management strategies may be used in teaching, learning leading towards better ways of delivering information to the learners in the classroom.

Finally, I shall explain what child psychology is? Every child stage development is important to influence his/her personal behavior when he/she grows up to be adult. So, child psychologists need to give opinions to their any ons child patient's partents and help their every child patient's patients to know why to teach their child/children in positive
teaching and learning way, when they are living at home daily. Because every child whose patients wll influence his/her behavior when he/she is adult and he /she needs to work in society.

For example, how to create or develop the child's unique skill or technique if the child is one one talent child to be needed to find whether he/she owns which kinds of skills , which
need their patients help him/her to discover. Then the child

can concentrate on training to upgrade the kind of undiscovered skills to hel him/her to become one talent child as well as attributing his/her human intelligence to our society's benefit. For another example, the educational psychologist needs to give opinions to the child's parents to teach
them how to persuade the child to follow learning disciplines to raise learning ability when they contact at home, the child ought first to be presented with problems and methods and only later with disciplines.

In conclusion, all of above these different kinds of psychologists, they have different professional psychological knowledge and skill to help our
social different stakeholder patients to solve their mental problems and satisfy their mental health service nees in order to let our society can
have many positive psychological mind people feel happy to live in our society.

Criminal behavioral psychological casing factors

In human society, human will do criminal behaviors easily in any time, whether what factors influences our moral mind is changed to immorality. In our societies, these crimes of the feeling that offended and threatened the general security in our societies. Crime is a changing concept, dependent upon the social development of a people, that is upon the fundamental interests and values dominating their common beliefes.In this chapter, I shall attempt to find the reasons and environments how and why they can persuade normal and common people to do criminal behaviors easily in any time. I aim to let my readers have more clear knowledge to know how any why their criminal behaviors are caused easily in any time.

There are two groups of factors lead to crime. One is ordinary factor and another is specific factors. Ordinary factors affect the whole of the society. Further secondary factors, such as geographical , sociological, physiological and atmospheric.

The society geographic factor elements play an important role. Geographical element affects the emotions and behavior of an individual. For example, one country's child individual murders are portortinally more in the period from January to April. In july, murders and total attacks are found to increase. Human needs change according to the changes in seasons, e.g. in winter in the European countries, the primaty basis needs increase and there are obstacles in satisfying their needs. The individuals have a tendency to criminal acts.

By geographical factors, it means to connect with physical environment. Due to geographical differences we find different types of culture and civilization in different geographical regions. Similarly deit, habbits and social organization will influence crime people choose to do different criminal behaviors.

Phsiological factors mean as a living being, man's physique and the functions of body are taken into consideration. A crime specialist is abnormality in the body and mind of a criminal right from his birth. Hence, he becomes a ciminallator in his life. A man of appressive and bad tempered mentality becomes a criminal easily. This inherited behavioralproperty is mainly responsible for the criminal attitude.

Some psychologists say that criminal behavior has its roots in the psychological set up of an individual. During the gradual psychological development of an individual, some mental weaknesses take shape. These weaknesses became the causes of criminal behavior. Mental instability and criminality are closely related. Disappointment, conflict,feeling of criminality, mental shocks etc. will be these criminal behavioral people's characteristics.

Circumstantial elements may include family circumstances factor, the family is looked upon as a powerful cause of forming good or bad personality developments. The very important task of a family is to socialize an individual and to impact social rules and to develop the individual culturally. So, that the individual becomes a responsible citizen. But, under certain circumstance this family responsibility fails and the members of the family tend to becomes criminals. Thse size of the family factormeans a big or a small family is respectively denoted by the number of members in the family. More members make a big family and fewer members make a small family.More members make a big family and fewer members make a small family.

Usually in a big family, there will be difficulties regarding food and management. In such large families, generally children tend to become criminals.

Discontendedness in the family factor means if the inter-relation between parents and children are not complacent, or instead of love, binding , sympathy , loyalty , co-operation,belief, dedication there are conflict easily, disbeliefs, selfishness, unreasonable behavior, rivalry in the family , then the members of the family especially the children behave in a dissatisfactory manner. From this, the criminal attitude arises.

Fallen family factor includes the person or persons of a family are involved in drinking, extra marital relations, polygamy and criminality. Absence of orderliness in the family means that the duty of the family guardians is to

be attentive towards the socially acceptable behavior of individuals and children in the family. They don't find time as they are involved in
their own duties. Further, they do not have desire or they are ignorant and they have undue or over belief in their children.

Whatever be the case, if the guardians do not care for the proper behavior of the children, then they will certainly turn towards criminal behaviors. Legally, crimes usually are defined as acts of omissions forbidden by law that can be punished by imprisonment and/or fine, e.g. murder, robbery, burglary, cape, drunken driving, child neglect, homicide and failure to pay
your taxes all are common examples.

The behavior definition at crime focuses on criminality , a certain personality profound that causes the most ararming sorts of crimes. All criminal behaviors involves the use of force, fraud, or stealing to obtain material or symbolic resources. They (the criminal behavioral doing people) have these similar characteristics. They usually feel indifference to the suffering and needs of others and low self-control. They have strategies to plan to do any criminal behaviors.

Thus, criminal behavior is the product of a systematic process that involves complex inter actions between individual, societies and ecological factors over the course of our lives.In other words, from conception onward the intellectual , emotional and physical attributes, we are developed one strongly influenced by our personal behaviors and physical processes, interactions with the physical environment, and interactions with other people, groups and institutions. These systematic processes affect the transmission from generation to generation of traits

associated
with increased involvment in crime.

www.ingramcontent.com/pod-product-compliance
Ingram Content Group UK Ltd.
Pitfield, Milton Keynes, MK11 3LW, UK
UKHW041844200726
13854UKWH00005BA/2051

9 798887 332802